THROUGH THE LENS

PÁDRAIG HARRINGTON'S THREE MAJOR VICTORIES

Foreword by Linton Walsh

Ireland Golf Digest

PUBLICATION

Published in 2008
by Walton Media
E7 Calmount Office Park
Ballymount
Dublin 12
Ireland

Printed in Singapore

THROUGH THE LENS is a collection of photographs compiled by Golf Digest Ireland Editorial Director Linton Walsh

First Edition

THROUGH THE LENS – PÁDRAIG HARRINGTON'S THREE MAJOR VICTORIES

ISBN 978-0-9560642-0-2

Dedicated to my parents Peter and Ann Walsh

AMONG MY RESPONSIBILITIES WITH GOLF DIGEST IRELAND is the photography we use in our magazines. We commission the best award-winning photographers from around the world and we search the world's largest photographic libraries on a daily basis.

Countless hours are spent selecting photography that captures the moment best, encapsulating the essence of the story, for that split second, to be immortalised forever. The best images are worth a thousand words and more when trying to convey to readers the tension and emotion inherent in our sport.

If imagery is my friend then space is my foe. Golf Digest Ireland covers so many different aspects of the game, written by the biggest names in golf, that we can only allocate so much space to each story.

Photographs are chosen to suit the story and the space on the page and as a result, all too often classic images don't see the light of day.

When Pádraig Harrington won the US PGA championship and claimed his third Major, I thought it would be a wonderful tribute, to tell the story again but in a way that no one had seen before.

Most of the photography in this book has never been published before, giving a unique insight into each of Pádraig Harrington's three Major victories. If you're anything like me, it will rekindle the fondest of memories from a truly special time in Irish golf, and indeed world sport as a whole.

Happy viewing,

Linton Walsh
Editorial Director
GolfDigest Ireland

First of three: Pádraig Harrington celebrates with his caddie Ronan Flood and the Claret Jug after winning The 136th Open Championship at the Carnoustie Golf Club in Carnoustie, Scotland.

In the pursuit of excellence there is no finish line.

CARNOUSTIE

THE 136th OPEN CHAMPIONSHIP

CARNOUSTIE GOLF LINKS

CARNOUSTIE, ANGUS, SCOTLAND

19th - 22nd JULY 2007

Aerial view over Carnoustie Golf Course with scenic views to the North Sea.

Aerial view of Carnoustie with clubhouse, Carnoustie Town and 'Barry Burn' snaking it's way through the course.

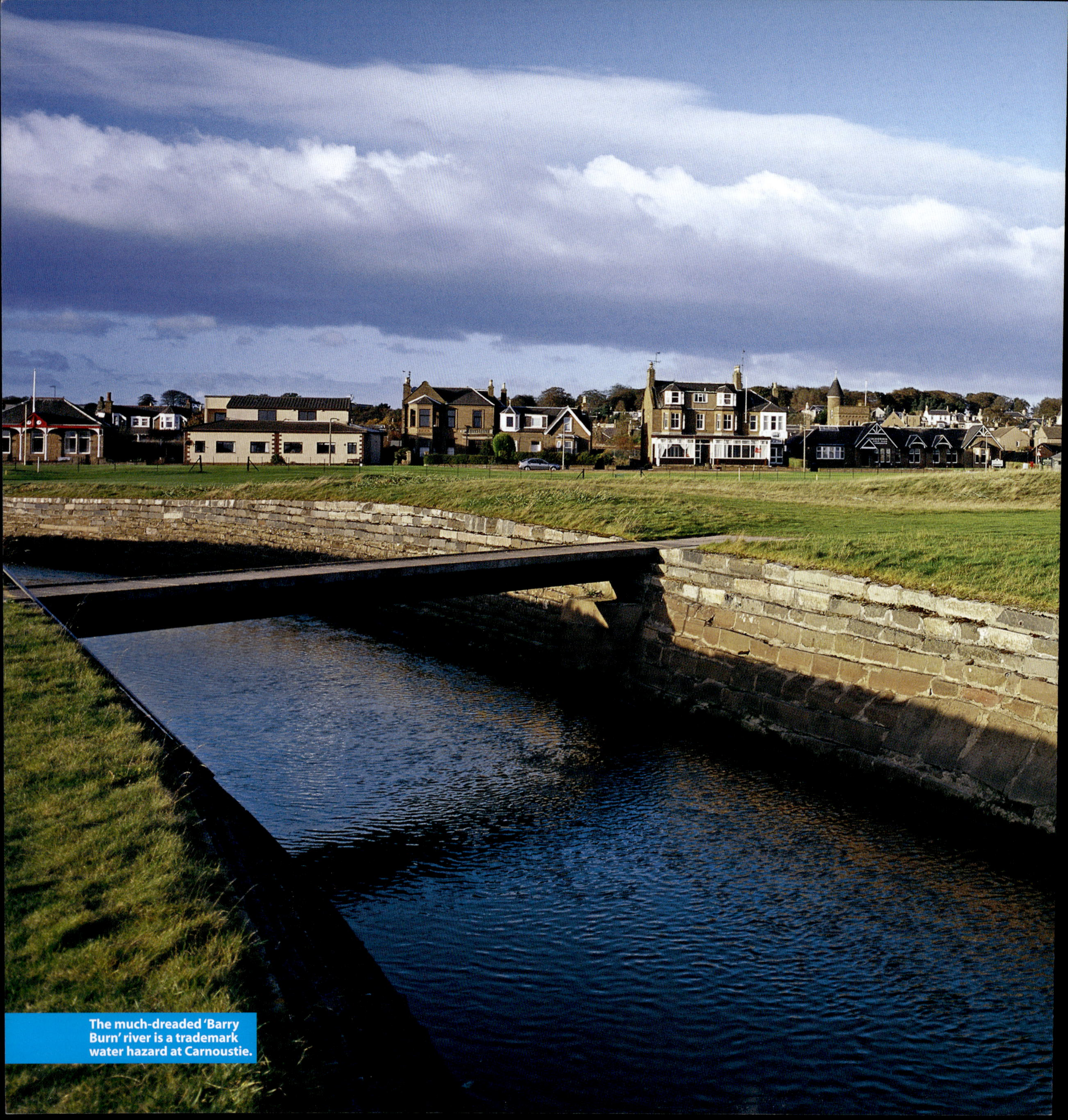

The much-dreaded 'Barry Burn' river is a trademark water hazard at Carnoustie.

Signing autographs for some fans during the first day practice rounds at Carnoustie.

Waiting with Paul McGinley during the first practice round.

Pádraig hits a shot on the second hole during the first round.

Pádraig in a relaxed mood as he walks across a green during the first round.

Pádraig's caddie Ronan cleans the ball before teeing off on the 13th hole during the second round.

Pádraig walks the 13th fairway during the second round.

Kartel
Kartel

Pádraig hits his tee shot on the 15th hole during the third round.

"I kept saying to people around me that I was convinced I was going to win the Open. It was like I was trying to tease myself, bringing the concept to the forefront of my mind so it wasn't such a lofty one, not so 'out there', if you like. Of course, deep down I didn't know I was going to win the Open. But I did know I couldn't do any more.

Watching a drive fly on the 9th hole during the final round.

Selecting a club with Ronan Flood during the final round.

Crossing the bridge at the 18th
with the scoreboard in view.

Sergio Garcia watches Pádraig's drive as they tee off on the first play-off hole.

"I'm very pleased with the score, I did a lot of good things all the way through. It's hard to lead a tournament like this for three or four days, so I'm in a good position and 69 is a good return. Just have to keep doing more of the same."

OXFORD
HOTELS & INNS
ROLEX

Close call: Chipping one over the 'Barry Burn' on the approach to the 18th green.

Sergio Garcia plays a bunker shot on the first play-off hole.

"The 18th is the toughest finishing hole in golf. There's trouble everywhere you look. I knew it was going to be tough for Sergio to make par. He did hit a lovely putt and I thought he had holed it."

The final moments for both players on the 18th green

History in the making: The gallery watch as Harrington sinks the winning putt.

It's there! The final putt at the 18th hole. Right; with caddie Ronan Flood.

HARRINGTON

Well played: Sergio Garcia congratulates Pádraig on his victory.

Pádraig hugs his son, Patrick, on the 18th green.

Kartel
Bank of Ireland

The agony and the ecstasy: Pádraig still can't believe it, while Sergio is left to ponder what could have been.

"It's going to take a long time for it to sink in. I know it was only a short putt, but the emotions of it ... I couldn't believe it as it was rolling in from right in the middle of the hole, and I'm thinking, 'The Open Champion."

Paul McGinley is quick to congratulate Pádraig on his win.

Pádraig celebrates with his wife Caroline, son Patrick and caddie Ronan Flood after defeating Sergio Garcia in the playoff.

adidas

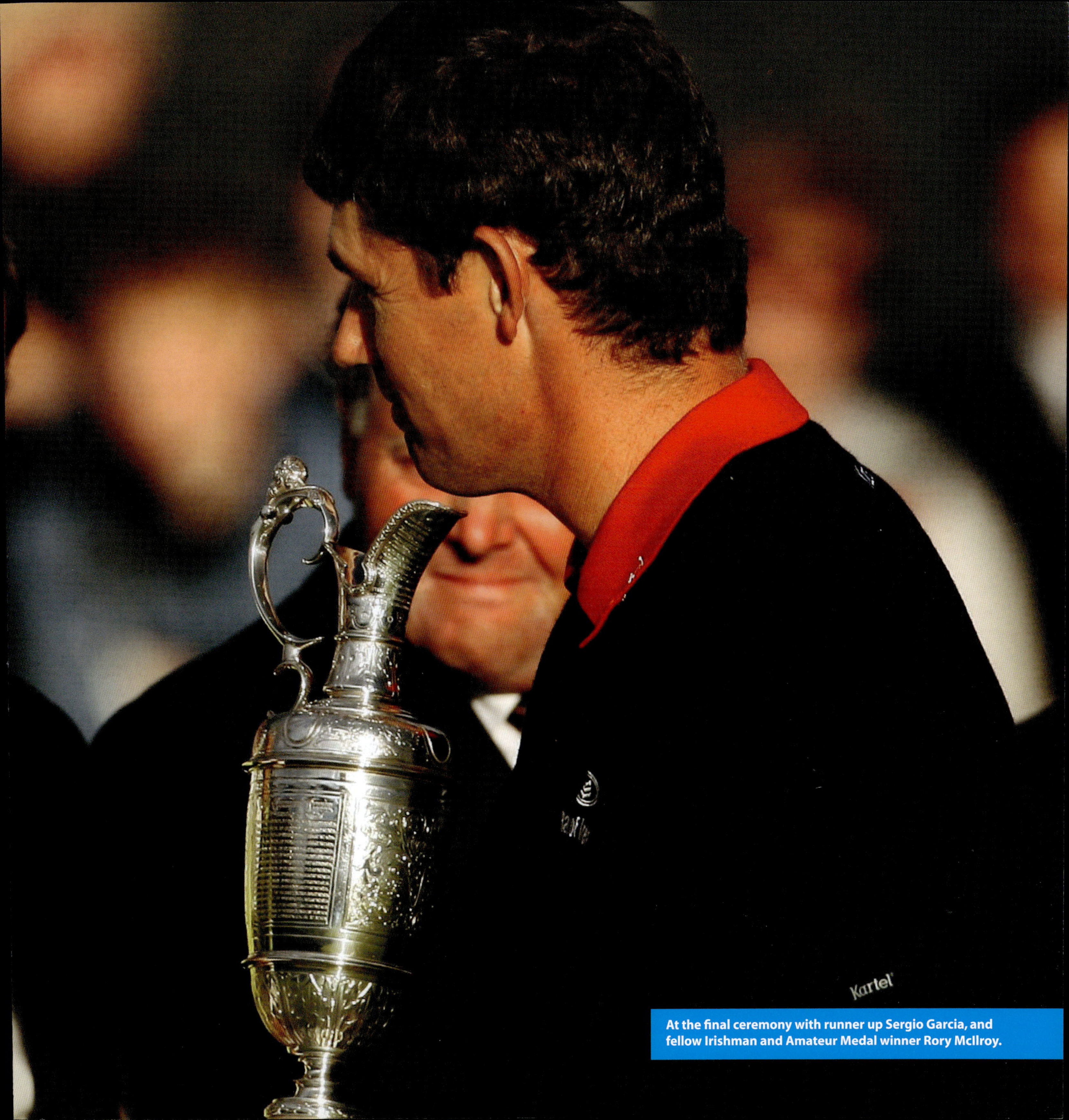

At the final ceremony with runner up Sergio Garcia, and fellow Irishman and Amateur Medal winner Rory McIlroy.

Staff

This one's for you! - Posing for the waiting media on the 18th green.

"There was so much going through my mind, some of it was genuine shock I had won the Open Championship".

The Champion in the 18th bunker with the press and (right) with the Claret Jug.

Wilson Staff

Wilson Staff
Kartel

Happy in the bunker: Posing with the Claret Jug for the assembled media.

"I have come a long way. When I turned pro I would have settled for becoming a journeyman. It's been great to be named as someone who could win a major. To actually go and do it, well I don't know what to think."

"I never let myself think I had blown the Open. If I had lost I would have struggled to come back out and be a professional golfer. It meant that much to me. It would have been incredibly hard to take".

It's a family affair: Pádraig celebrates with his wife Caroline and mother Breda.

Pádraig is all smiles as he poses with the Claret Jug

A very prophetic message: The final scores at Carnoustie with the "See you at Royal Birkdale" message.

With his son Patrick and the Claret Jug as he speaks with the media.

Wilson Staff
OPEN
Kartel

Press gang: From left to right; Karl MacGinty, Charlie Mulqueen, Philip Reid, Greg Allen, Padraig Harrington and Brian Keogh.

R&A
THE OPEN
CHAMPIONSHIP
Wilson Staff
Kartel
Bank of Ireland
NO MOBILE PHONES

Pádraig drinks from the Claret Jug at Carnoustie following his victory. Right; with wife Caroline.

Kartel

Bringing home the bacon! Arriving at Weston Airport with the Claret Jug.

Wilson Staff
FM104
TODAY fm
TODAY fm
RTE

The Irish media get the first shots of their new Champion.

Wilson Staff

Pádraig shows off the Claret Jug at Stackstown.

Pádraig with fans and fellow members at Stackstown Golf Club in Dublin.

LADY PRESIDENT

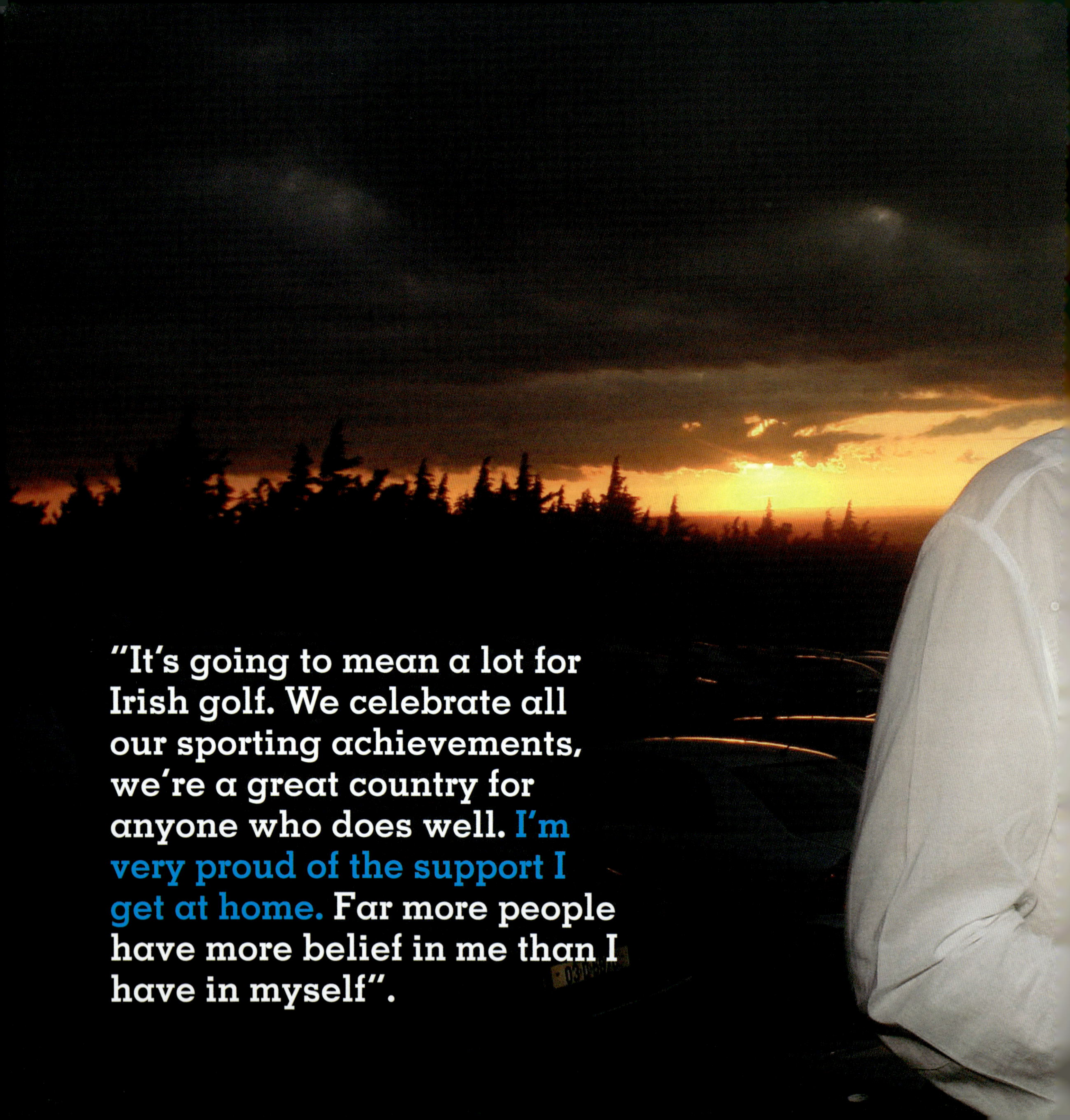

"It's going to mean a lot for Irish golf. We celebrate all our sporting achievements, we're a great country for anyone who does well. **I'm very proud of the support I get at home.** Far more people have more belief in me than I have in myself".

ROYAL BIRKDALE

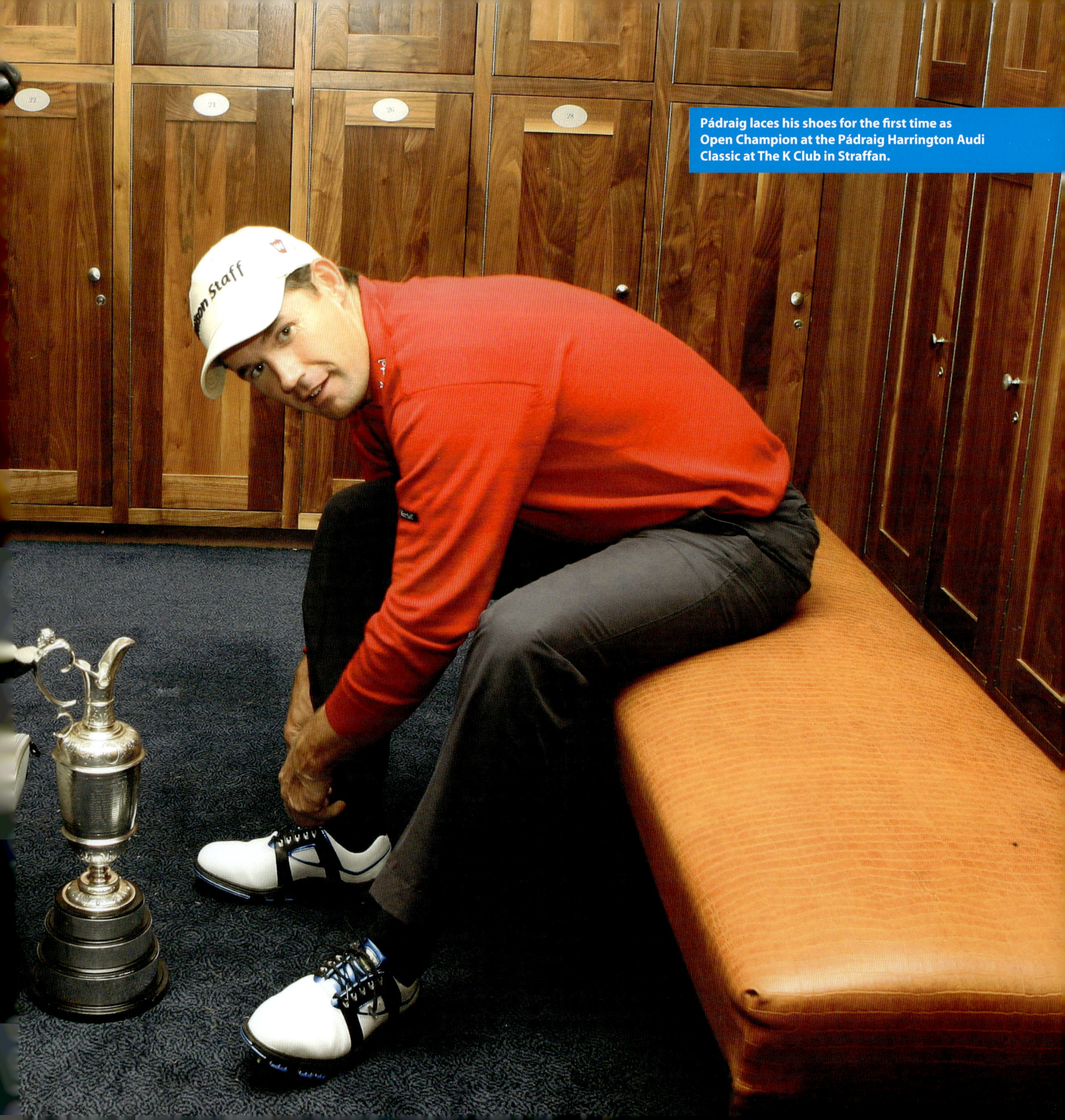

Pádraig laces his shoes for the first time as Open Champion at the Pádraig Harrington Audi Classic at The K Club in Straffan.

I am now the Open Champion of 2007 forever more. It feels great to say it. Since the putt went in I have been on cloud nine, it has been one big party and I don't want it to stop.

THE 137th OPEN CHAMPIONSHIP

ROYAL BIRKDALE GOLF CLUB

SOUTHPORT, ENGLAND

17th - 20th JULY 2008

The new green on the 572-yard, par-5 17th (foreground) is squeezed between dunes, and the wishbone fairway of the 473-yard, par-4 18th offers a members' par-5 down the left.

As befitting one of the globe's great par- 3s, the 184-yard 12th sits in resplendent isolation.

The L-shape drainage ditch serves as a gutter on the bowling-alley fairway of the 499-yard, par-4 13th.

In a relaxed mood during the first day's practice at Royal Birkdale. Right: On the range during the first day's practice.

Staff
Bank of Ireland
Kartel

Getting out of trouble: Pádraig chips from the sand and lines up a putt at the 2nd hole during round three.

Wilson Staff
Bank of Ireland

Signing some autographs during the 3rd practice round.

Wilson Staff
Kartel
Bank of Ireland

Tending to his wrist problem during the 3rd practice round.

"If it wasn't the Open I would have pulled out. I would have come for treatment and then decided I could not risk it. But because it's Open week I will definitely make the effort."

- Pádraig talks to the press regarding his wrist injury

Wilson Staff
Kartel
Bank of Ireland

THE OPEN
PRESS
PRESS
THE OPEN
PRESS

Walking the course with some of the press (from left; Philip Reid, Brian Keogh, Charlie Mulqueen and Karl MacGinty) during the 3rd practice round.

"This is a really pleasant golf course for everybody. I can understand why a lot of players would rate it very highly. It's not tricky, there's nothing funky about it. Everything is there in front of you. I'd say it's more like Portmarnock than Royal Portrush, which is trickier. This is much, much more straightforward than that".

Wilson Staff

Pádraig hits a shot from the rough during the first round.

"I prefer a difficult test because it limits the number of people who can compete on the golf course. If there's more pressure on you, the decision-making gets tested, so under those circumstances, it might be better when the decision-making is reasonably straightforward, as it is on this golf course".

Testing conditions: On the 11th tee on the first day.

Pádraig acknowledges the crowd on the 18th green during the first round.

Pádraig is watched by spectators as he plays a difficult shot on the 11th during the second round.

"When we started, we were feeling very sorry for ourselves and then the wind suddenly changed to make things even tougher. All of a sudden I'm starting to leak a few shots and wondered what the cut is".

adidas
cobra
view from.

Pádraig salutes the crowd alongside caddie Ronan Flood as they walk down the 18th fairway during the second round.

Wilson Staff
THE OPEN
CHAMPIONSHIP
HARRINGTON
Wilson Staff

Pádraig ponders his next shot on the 8th during the second round.

Pádraig Ireland gestures to the camera during the second round.

When the going gets tough... Pádraig plays out of a bunker on the 2nd hole during the third round.

Pádraig picks up on the 5th green at a windswept Birkdale.

The wind during the Open tested many players mettle. Pádraig's hat is blown off in a gust at the 4th green during the third round.

"That was one of **the toughest sets of conditions** I've experienced."

- Pádraig remarking on the high winds that swept through Birkdale during the Championship

Bank of Ireland

Wilson

Pádraig plays an approach shot to the 6th during the third round.

"Very few people have won back-to-back majors. Coming into this week I was trying to play that down but winning a second one does set you apart. There are less people in that club".

THE OPEN CHAMPIONSHIP
UNISYS
UNISYS
HOLE PAR PLAYER
39 −1 CHOI
39 +2 NORMAN
42 +2 HARRINGTON
40 +3 VILLEGAS
40 +3 FURYK
41 +4 ALLENBY
43 +4 APPLEBY
AFTER 6
GAME ROUND PLAYER CUML.
39 NOREN
ALLENBY
+10
+2

Pádraig putts on the 7th green as David Duval of USA looks on during the third round.

"I never at any stage started to think about what it means to win a second Open, or if I did, I stopped myself".

Greg Norman (R) of Australia and Pádraig Harrington in action on the 5th green during the fourth round.

"I did tell him coming down 18, that I was sorry it wasn't his story that would be told this evening. I did feel that ... but I wanted to win it myself, too".

- Pádraig on fellow competitor Greg Norman's gutsy attempt to make history by winning the Open Championship at 53 years of age

Pádraig Harrington's name card is added to the main scoreboard during the final round.

NGT

On the approach to the 18th green - and a place in sporting history.

The final approach at the 18th fairway.

It's in the bag. Ronan Flood congratulates Pádraig on his second Major title.

Arguably the most satisfying final putt of Pádraig's career to date.

Wilson

A heart-felt congratulations from The Shark, Greg Norman. Right; 'We did it again!' - with Ronan Flood at the 18th green.

HARRINGTON

Greg 'The Shark' Norman congratulates Pádraig's family on his victory at Royal Birkdale.

"I did feel like I could win many more Majors - but for it to happen so quickly was a big bonus. My story is still unfolding so it's not the time to sit back and look at it - it's time to keep moving forward and keep playing. I'll get nostalgic hopefully in 30 years time".

Pádraig receives the Claret Jug from Dennis Watson, Captain of The Royal Birkdale Golf Club.

At the winners table. Also pictured (1st from right) are Ian Poulter, runner up and Chris Wood (2nd from right) who won the Amateurs Medal.

Pádraig holds the Claret Jug with the Royal Birkdale clubhouse in the background.

"You have to look at it like this, it's about averages. You get yourself in position enough times, it will fall on the right side of you some of the times, and the wrong side some of the times. The key is to get into position".

Staff

Pádraig celebrates with the Claret Jug with son Patrick after winning by 4 strokes.

"This was uncharted territory for me as I don't normally make it this easy. I am normally sweating over a four footer not having a casual walk down the last and five putts to win!"

oceanico
GROUP

Wilson
oceânico
GROUP
kartel

Kissing the silverware once again.

"I've improved and I'm continuing to improve. I've got to say that if you ask me my best trait over the years it's been my ability to learn. To look around me, see what's out there, take the best from everything and try and put it together".

Here we go again! - The Harringtons line up for more photographs.

Nikon
PHOTO
Nikon
PHOTO
Nikon
PHOTO

A familiar sight! Pádraig with the claret jug, wife Caroline and son Patrick and recent addition Ciaran. Right: with proud mother Breda.

Wilson Staff

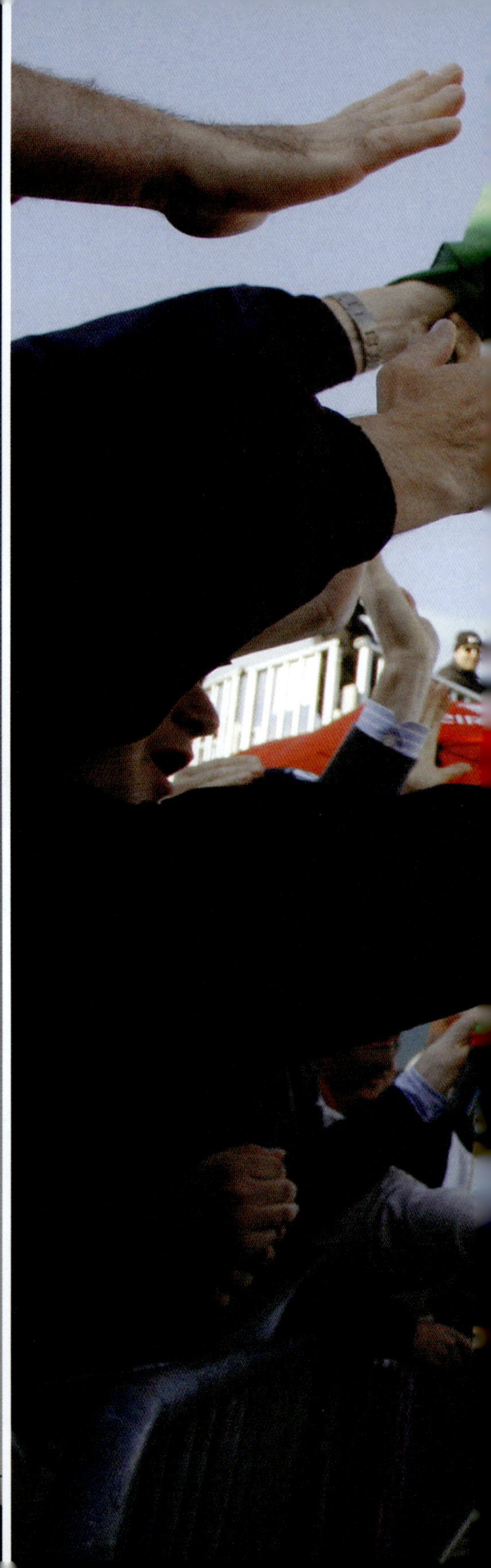

Pádraig poses with the trophy and (right) is congratulated by travelling Irish fans

Bank of Ireland
Kartel

Titleist
Wilson Staff
Kartel
THE OPEN

Pádraig with Bob Rotella (left) and Bob Torrance (right).

"I said to my caddie there's no better experience than walking down the 18th on Sunday at The Open - well I told a lie - there was a better experience - leading and winning the Open when the gallery is full and cheering for you".

The scene is now set for The Open at Turnberry in 2009.

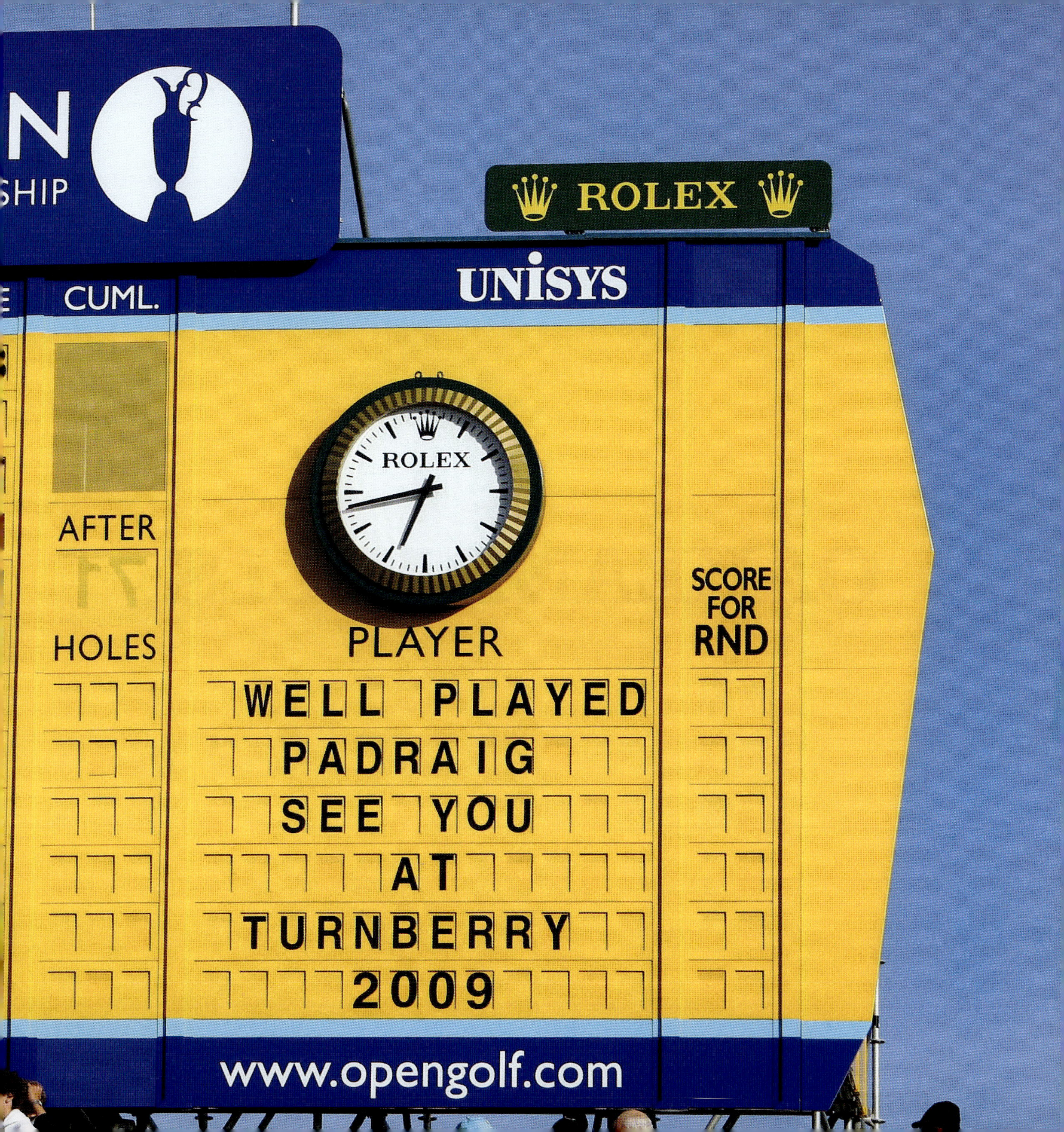
N
SHIP
ROLEX
UNISYS
CUML.
ROLEX
AFTER
HOLES
PLAYER
SCORE FOR RND
WELL PLAYED
PADRAIG
SEE YOU
AT
TURNBERRY
2009
www.opengolf.com

OAKLAND HILLS

THE 90th PGA CHAMPIONSHIP

OAKLAND HILLS COUNTRY CLUB

BLOOMFIELD TOWNSHIP, MICHIGAN

7th - 10th AUGUST 2008

The 238-yard 17th hole (right foreground) is one example of Oakland Hills' difficult greens.

The 18th green at Oakland Hills.

Pádraig hits a drive off the 4th tee during a practice round.

Pádraig takes on the caddie's role during a practice round.

Pádraig signs autographs for American fans at Oakland Hills.

Pádraig reaches for the hat of five-year old Maui Baba of Michigan to sign an autograph.

Pádraig plays from a bunker during a practice round.

Wilson Staff

Pádraig speaks to the media after playing his practice round.

Pádraig tees off at the first hole during the first round.

Pádraig watches a drive during the first round.

Pádraig tees off on the 12th hole during the opening round.

Pádraig plays from a bunker on the eighth hole during round two.

Pádraig and an official look through a fence for Harrington's ball on the eighth hole during round two.

"I've won many a tournament where I felt I wasn't swinging as well as I could; and performed poorly sometimes when I felt I was swinging well. "So I'm a bit, a little bit of a contrast like that."

Pádraig plays a shot on the 12th hole during round two.

HARRINGTON
PGA

Pádraig waves to the gallery after making a putt on the 2nd green during the third round.

Pádraig watches his tee shot on the sixth hole during the third round.

Wilson Staff
TaylorMade
Kartel

Pádraig Harrington (L) of Ireland, Sergio Garcia (C) of Spain and Charlie Wi (R) of the US approach their balls on the first green during the final round.

"It was totally different from The Open, I was very comfortable with my game at The Open".

Wilson Staff
Kartel

Pádraig lines up his putt on the first green during the final round.

Pádraig and caddie Ronan Flood walk down the fairway on the 10th hole during the completion of round three.

"My co-ordination was out all week. On Thursday and Friday I couldn't get to the clubhouse quick enough. My game was going downhill very quickly out on the golf course. When I went back and had a look at it, and had a discussion with my trainer at home; it was possible that I was dehydrated. And that's what caused the lack of co-ordination".

Wilson Staff

oceanico
Wilson

Pádraig plays his second shot on the 12th hole during the final round.

Pádraig plays his third shot to the 12th hole during the final round.

Pádraig and Sergio Garcia look on from the tee on the 14th hole during the final round.

"I love the idea of the back nine of a major on a Sunday. I love it so much that I'm actually disappointed I'm seven months away from the next Major, and I don't know what I'm going to do."

Kartel
Kartel
adidas

"I've really focused hard on the majors the last two years. My whole schedule is built around majors. And definitely I've turned up at other events, and unless I get into contention, you know, sometimes it feels like a race, like a sprint, whereas a major feels like a marathon. I feel like I can be patient and take my time. And I love the feeling of knowing that it's going to come down to the back nine; it's going to come down to who can do it under pressure in the last nine holes."

Pádraig swaps clubs with his caddie Ronan Flood to play his third shot on the 14th green during the final round.

Pádraig reacts to his par putt on the 16th hole.

Pádraig plays his tee shot on the 17th hole during the final round.

Pádraig and his caddie Ronan Flood look up at the rain during the final round.

Sergio Garcia reacts as his shot from the 18th fairway lands in a bunker during the final round.

Pádraig reacts to his birdie shot on the 17th hole by holding up his ball alongside Sergio Garcia

"I really felt good out there, a beaming. I hit the ball probably every bit as solid as I've ever hit it".

Wilson Staff
Bank of Ireland

Pádraig plays from a bunker in the fairway of the 18th hole during the final round.

"I think I was willing them into the hole at that stage. You have to get focused and give it a go."

Wilson

Pádraig plays his second shot on the 18th hole during the final round.

"That's a nice question to ask. It's a good situation if you can ask that question - it's a big step."

- Pádraig reacts to a reporter's question if he can challenge to become the World's best golfer

Pádraig putts to make par and seal victory on the 18th hole during the final round.

Staff

Pádraig celebrates with a fist pump after making par on the 18th hole during the final round.

Bank of Ireland
Kartel

The packed grandstands look on as Pádraig punches the air in celebration.

GA CHAMPIONSHIP
HARRINGTON
VIVA

PGA
Bank of Ireland

Waving to the crowd on the 18th green. Left; Three's a charm; Pádraig high fives Ronan Flood after bagging his third major.

Sergio Garcia of Spain and Pádraig shake hands after completing the final round.

Bank of Ireland

These lips are well used to kissing silverware at this stage! - Pádraig with the PGA Championship trophy.

"I really do like the fact that no other European has won two Majors consecutively, though, because obviously I hold a lot of European players who I grew up watching in high esteem. To believe that I achieved something that they hadn't is very special."

Pádraig celebrates with his wife Caroline, caddie Ronan Flood and two Children.

Wilson Staff

Pádraig talks to the media during a press conference after winning the 90th PGA Championship at Oakland Hills Country Club on 10th August, 2008.

"This is a different win. I was comfortable with my game in winning the Open. This week I haven't been as confident and comfortable. Here I hit some of the wildest golf shots ever hit on a golf course on Friday. But I knew I had the ability to win if I got a chance. In the end it was a lot of sheer willpower (that won it)."

PGA
www.pga.com
Wilson Staff
PGA
PGA
Kartel
Bank of Ireland

Wilson Staff
HOLE
LEADERS
PAR

Pádraig holds the trophy after winning the 90th PGA Championship at Oakland Hills Country Club on 10th August, 2008 in Bloomfield Township, Michigan.

With the PGA Championship trophy and caddie Ronan Flood.

Staff
Bank of Ireland
ANNUAL
MPIONSHIP
OF THE
FESSIONAL
GOLFERS
SOCIATION
OF
MERICA
AN WANAMAKER
TROPHY

Wilson
oceanico
GROUP
ANNUAL
CHAMPIONSHIP
OF THE
PROFESSIONAL
GOLFERS
ASSOCIATION
OF
AMERICA
RODMAN WANAMAKER
TROPHY
TIGER WOODS
PHIL MICKELSON
TIGER WOODS
2006 MEDINAH C.C
TIGER WOODS
2007 SOUTHERN HILLS C.C

Homeward bound; Pádraig ends a fine season, with the Claret Jug and US PGA trophy.

IRELAND'S BIGGEST SELLING GOLF MAGAZINE

FREE GOLF MAGAZINE FREE GOLF BALLS FREE GOLF CAP FREE POSTAGE

12 ISSUES ONLY €75/£60

CALL NOW +353 (1) 4199604

MasterCard VISA LASER